DISCOVER
Use Your Gifts and Help Others Find Theirs

Joel Comiskey

Published by CCS Publishing

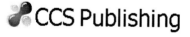 CCS Publishing

www.joelcomiskeygroup.com

Published by CCS Publishing
23890 Brittlebush Circle
Moreno Valley, CA 92557 USA
1-888-344-CELL

Cover design by Josh Talbot
Editing by Scott Boren

Library of Congress Control Number: 2007900318

CCS Publishing is the book-publishing division of Joel Comiskey Group, a resource and
coaching ministry dedicated to equipping leaders for cell-based ministry.
Find us on the World Wide Web at **www.joelcomiskeygroup.com**

Publisher's Cataloging-in-Publication
(Provided by Quality Books, Inc.)

    Comiskey, Joel, 1956-
      Discover : use your gifts and help others find theirs
    / by Joel Comiskey.
      p. cm.
      Includes bibliographical references and index.
      LCCN 2007900318
      ISBN-13: 978-0979067921
      ISBN-10: 0979067928

      1. Fruit of the Spirit. 2. Ability. 3. Church group
    work. 4. Self-actualization (Psychology)--Religious
    aspects--Christianity. I. Title.

    BV4501.3.C6552 2008   248.4
                       QBI07-600237

Table of Contents

Introduction

How often have we longed to be like someone else? "I wish I was a great conversationalist like Tom. He always has something interesting to say, but when I'm in a group of people, my brain freezes up, and I can hardly remember what to say." Or "I wish I could teach like Donna. She articulates her message so perfectly. In comparison, my teaching is simplistic and even superficial." You might even have prayed at some point, "Lord, make me like . . . ."

Too many of us stumble through life with an inferiority complex. We don't think we're special or smart. We don't think we have much to offer God.

The good news is that God has made you unique. He has gifted you and given you a particular place in his body, the church. Romans 12:6 says that "We have different gifts, according to the grace given us."[1]

I hope to plainly show you in the following pages what the gifts are and how to discover your own unique gift. My goal is for you to discover and start using your gift(s) before you have completed the book.

I would encourage you to be involved in a church-sponsored small group. The atmosphere of fellowship and trust in a small group makes the free flow of the spiritual gifts possible. When trust is established, people are more willing to risk and try out new, potential gifts. A cell group can provide honest feedback about the person's efforts, as well as areas for improvement.

---

[1] Unless otherwise noted, all Scripture is taken from the HOLY BIBLE, NEW INTERNATIONAL VERSION®. Copyright © 1973, 1978, 1984 by International Bible Society. Used by permission of Zondervan Publishing House. All rights reserved.

Additional Resources

Discover is part of a two book advanced training series that prepares someone to become a mature follower of Jesus Christ. The other book currently in this series is *Coach*, a resource for helping leaders coach developing leaders.

The Basic Training Series is comprised of five books, which are available at www.joelcomiskeygroup.com or by calling toll free 1-888-344-CELL.

You can use this book individually, in a small group setting, or in a classroom.

Teaching outlines and PowerPoints for these two advanced equipping books and all five books of the Basic Training Series are on CD. This CD can be purchased at the JCG web site or by calling the toll free number above.

A more in-depth book on the gifts of the Spirit called *The Spirit-filled Small Group* is available. In that book I go into more detail about the use of the spiritual gifts in the context of small group ministry. This book, in contrast, is the training manual that will help you apply what is written in *The Spirit-filled Small Group*. Both books are available at www.joelcomiskeygroup.com or by calling 1-888-344-CELL.

The Holy Spirit and You

As I write on my balcony here in Moreno Valley, California, a strong wind is blowing. The trees are swaying and my umbrella is rocking back and forth. The wind here in Moreno Valley is fierce and can knock down trees and backyard tables. I've even seen it move my heavy basketball pole six feet. I've learned from experience that when it really starts blowing, it's best to be inside.

I've never actually seen the wind. I only witness its powerful effects. Like the wind, no human has ever seen the Holy Spirit. Jesus, on the other hand, came in bodily form and lived among people. His disciples and others lived with him for about three years. When Jesus died and rose again, he left the invisible Holy Spirit to continue the work he started.

When describing the Holy Spirit, Jesus actually used the wind as an example of the Holy Spirit's invisible power, "The wind blows wherever it pleases. You hear its sound, but you cannot tell where it comes from or where it is going. So it is with everyone born of the Spirit" (John 3:8, NIV).

Even though no one has ever seen the Holy Spirit, the Bible tells us a lot about his personality—one that we can know and understand.

The Holy Spirit Is a Person

A survey taken of U.S. residents showed that 61% agreed with the statement that the Holy Spirit is "a symbol of God's presence or power, but is not a living entity."

Why do so many believe that the Holy Spirit is non-living or symbolic? I'm sure at least one reason is the proliferation of films and books that portray impersonal forces competing with each other for the souls of men and women. The film *Star Wars* is just one example. Like the characters in the movie *Star Wars,* many simply consider the Holy Spirit to be a "good force." As the personal presence of God, the Spirit is not merely some force or influence. The living God is a God of power; and by the Spirit the power of the living God is present with us and for us.

Try IT!

What has been your understanding of the Holy Spirit's personhood up to this point?

_____

_____

People also more readily identify with the concept of God the Father and Jesus Christ the Son because the imagery of father and son is more obvious to us. The Holy Spirit is harder to grasp. People, in fact, tend to call the Spirit "it" rather than "He." Why? Because people find it hard to imagine the Holy Spirit as a "person."

Try IT!

Read Hebrews 3:7.
What does God tell us to do here?

_____

_____

How do you know/sense when God is speaking to you?

_____

_____

_____

The Bible describes the Holy Spirit as a person who knows, feels, and wills. Like a person, the Holy Spirit searches and guides. In Ephesians 4:30, Paul wrote: "Do not grieve the Holy Spirit of God, with whom you were sealed for the day of redemption." We can only cause grief or make a person sad. Scripture speaks of the Holy Spirit's mind, his love and his instruction.[1]

Try IT!

Read Ephesians 4:30.
What trait of the Holy Spirit's personality do you see in this verse?

_____

_____

Confess to God and ask for his forgiveness for any area in your life in which you are grieving the Holy Spirit.

_____

_____

_____

Besides his personhood, the Holy Spirit is God. He's one in essence with the Father and the Son, but he's also a distinct person. We call the Holy Spirit the "third person of the Trinity." Many Scriptures point to this fact. All the attributes of God are also descriptive of the Holy Spirit as well. When we talk about the Holy Spirit, God the Father, and Jesus the Son we are not talking about three Gods. We are talking about one God in three persons with unique functions.

---

[1] The Holy Spirit is called God (1 Corinthians 2:11; 2 Corinthians 3:17; Acts 5:3-4); He possesses divine attributes, such as omniscience (1 Corinthians 2:10-11), omnipresence (Psalm 139:7) and omnipotence (Zechariah 4:6); He's the third person of the Trinity (Matthew 28:19). For more on this topic, see René Pache, *The Person and Work of the Holy Spirit* (Chicago, Ill.: Moody Press, 1954), pp. 14-19.

Try IT!

Read Matthew 28:19.
How did Jesus instruct his disciples to baptize converts?

_____

_____

Write out in your own words how you understand the Trinity.

_____

_____

_____

_____

_____

What Is the Filling of the Spirit?

After Jesus died on the cross, the disciples were confused. They didn't know what to do; they felt abandoned and helpless. They huddled together, fearing for their own safety. When Jesus appeared to them after his resurrection, he drove away their fears and doubts. Freedom reigned.

But instead of telling his disciples to immediately go everywhere and proclaim the gospel, Jesus said, "Do not leave Jerusalem, but wait for the gift my Father promised, which you have heard me speak about. For John baptized with water, but in a few days you will be baptized with the Holy Spirit" (Acts 1:4–5). The rest of the book of Acts records the Holy Spirit's mighty work through the early followers of Jesus. The works of the Holy Spirit continue today. He has not changed. The Holy Spirit desires to work with power in your life, just as he did in the lives of the early disciples.

The scripture says that we need to be filled with the Holy Spirit. Ephesians 5:18 says, "Do not get drunk on wine, which leads to debauchery. Instead, be filled with the Spirit." In the original Greek, the phrase be filled is actually a present-tense continuous verb. To signify a "one-time filling," Paul would have used the past tense or a future verb tense; instead, he chose the present tense to denote that the filling of the Holy Spirit is not a one-time event, but a continual experience. The scripture says that we must be continually filled with the Spirit, not just once or twice.

The word filling might seem awkward when referring to one way the Holy Spirit works in us. The Spirit of God is not a liquid, like water. Because the Holy Spirit is a person, it makes sense to talk about the Holy Spirit's leading or direction in our lives.

Holy Spirit led is a good way to look at the Holy Spirit's guidance in our lives. A person who is filled with the Spirit is led by the Spirit—directed in a gentle, loving way. Spirit-led people allow the Holy Spirit to direct and guide their decisions, plans and activities. Because the world, the flesh and the devil oppose the Spirit-led lifestyle, we need to be filled and renewed continually.

Try IT!

Read Acts 2:1-13 and 4:31.
How many times were the disciples filled with the Spirit in these passages? (and many more times afterwards)

_____

_____

In your opinion, why does a person need to be filled with the Spirit more than once?

_____

_____

_____

_____

I remember the evening in 1974 when the Spirit first filled me. I was transformed and empowered. I received a new perspective and boldness. Yet, that first filling wasn't enough. I needed more fillings after that. Acts chapter two talks about the Holy Spirit's coming on the day of Pentecost and the initial filling of the Holy Spirit in the 120 disciples. But just two chapters later the believers needed another filling (Acts 4:31). The initial filling in Acts chapter two wasn't enough to empower the disciples throughout their lives on earth. We too need to be continually filled with the Holy Spirit. And as he fills us, we then will walk in the Spirit and honor God by the way that we live. At the same time, empowered by the very presence of God living in us, we will be a blessing to those around us.

Try IT!

Read Ephesians 5:18.
How does the apostle Paul describe the filling of the Spirit in this verse?

_____

_____

How many fillings with the Holy Spirit have you received? If your answer is, "none," read the following section and then pray, asking the Holy Spirit to fill you.

_____

_____

_____

_____

When I was first filled with the Holy Spirit, I noticed I had a new boldness to witness to others. The power to witness to others was the main evidence that I was filled with the Holy Spirit. Others feel a warm sense of God's love. Some don't feel anything. Others might speak in unknown languages (Acts 2). I don't believe any one experience is required evidence of having been filled with the Holy Spirit. In other words, you don't need to speak in tongues, shake, or weep in order to prove you've been filled with the Holy Spirit. Yet, you might experience all these things.

How to be Filled with the Spirit

I know of no magical formula to be filled with the Holy Spirit. I do know that Scripture says in Luke 11:13, "If you then, though you are evil, know how to give good gifts to your children, how much more will your Father in heaven give the Holy Spirit to those who ask him!"

Just ask God. He wants to fill you. He wants to work powerfully in your life, and he is able to do so.

Some people make long lists of do's and don'ts that must be completed before God will give his Holy Spirit. While some of those suggestions are commendable (such as, confession of sin and commitment to obedience—see Acts 5:32), long lists often give the false appearance of an unwilling God who is playing hide and seek with his people.

The scripture is plain and simple here. If you ask the Holy Spirit to fill you, He will. If you don't ask you won't receive. It's as simple as that.

Do IT!
Ask the Holy Spirit to fill you now.

Be sure to confess any known sin to God that might hinder you from experiencing the filling of the Holy Spirit. If you will come before God in a humble way, confessing your sin and asking him to fill you with the Holy Spirit, expect that he will.

He is a gracious and loving God. He wants to give great gifts to his children. And, he longs to fill you right now!

Remember IT!

What truth from this lesson impacted you the most?

_____

_____

_____

_____

_____

_____

Main points:
1. The Holy Spirit is a person who can think, act, and feel.
2. The Trinity means there is one God who exists in three persons: Father, Son, and Holy Spirit.
3. The filling of the Spirit is not just a one-time event. Believers should be filled continually.

Apply IT!
1. Treat the Holy Spirit as a person—feel his presence, talk to him, listen to him, and worship him.
2. Ask the Holy Spirit to fill you daily.
3. Live each day in humble dependence on the Holy Spirit.

The Holy Spirit and the Gifts of the Body of Christ

n 1995, I was the special guest speaker at a church in Big Bear, California. I had just finished preaching and was standing in the reception area listening to the pastor close the service. I felt a freezing draft of air coming from a window behind me. This particular window was one of those old drop-down windows that had a latch at the top and a thin metal edge surrounding the glass. I used my left hand to unlatch the lever at the top and wham, the window fell downward like a guillotine. It fell so fast that I didn't have time to remove my right pointer finger. The metal edge sliced right through my finger and I could literally see one end dangling by the bone.

I winced in pain and ran to get some help. Thankfully, a nearby emergency center stitched my finger back together. What a day!

In the following months, I realized afresh how much I needed that right finger to perform even the smallest tasks around the house. My other body parts had to work overtime to perform even menial tasks. I was painfully reminded that each part of my body is essential.

We Need Each Other

The Bible tells us that we are part of Christ's body. We are totally dependent on each other under Jesus Christ. Paul the apostle says, "God has combined the members of the body and has given greater honor to the parts that lacked it, so that there should be no division in the body, but that its parts should have equal concern for each other. If one part suffers, every part suffers with it; if one part is honored, every part rejoices with it (1 Corinthians 12: 24–26).

How do you know what part of the body you are? You know by the gift God has given you (1 Corinthians 12). All gifts are necessary for the body to work properly. And no member is inferior to another. Why? Because the way the body works is that those who at first seem inferior are given greater honor, so as to remove the possibility of dissension. Ephesians 4 puts it like this: "speaking the truth in love, we will in all things grow up into him who is the Head, that is, Christ. From him the whole body, joined and held together by every supporting ligament, grows and builds itself up in love, as each part does its work" (4:15–16).

We need each other. Your contribution is just as important as the finger to the hand or the leg to the foot. When each of us is using our gift, the body functions normally. The opposite is also true. If a part of the body is not functioning, the rest feel it. Meeting together in both the cell (small group) and celebration (large group) is necessary to use the gifts and minister to one another. Hebrews 10:24 says, "Let us not give up meeting together, as some are in the habit of doing, but let us encourage one another—and all the more as you see the Day approaching."

As you discover your spiritual gift, you'll understand what part you play in the body of Christ.

Try IT!

Read 1 Corinthians 12: 3-26.
How does Paul connect the relationship between parts of the body and the gifts of the Spirit?

_____

_____

Do you feel intimately connected to believers in your church or cell group? Why or why not?

_____

_____

_____

Charismatic

I was talking to a friend about Jim, a youth leader who regularly speaks on university campuses. "Jim is so charismatic," my friend said. "And what I mean by that is he has a very charismatic personality." Then my friend added, "Jim is also charismatic because he believes in all the gifts of the Spirit." I've had similar conversations in which the word charismatic needed clarification.

The word charisma in the English language refers to a magnetic personality—the ability to inspire enthusiasm, interest, or affection in others by means of personal charm or influence.

Yet, the original meaning of the word charismatic comes from the Greek language. It literally means gift and the word is *charismata*. Interestingly enough, the Greek word for grace is *charis*.

God's gifts are his grace to his church. Some writers have referred to God's gifts as gracelets. God's gracelets energize and build up Christ's church.

Try IT!

Read 1 Corinthians 12:4.
The Greek word *charismata* is used for our English word "gift" in this verse.
Share in your own words what you understand between the relationship between God's gifts (*charismata*) and God's grace (*charis*).

_____

_____

_____

_____

_____

_____

_____

Each part has a job

My nephew, Grayson, is part of a Christian rock band called Ives. Grayson recently went on a two-month tour with Ives. We were amazed at all the daily tasks and behind the scenes work that takes place. Each member of the band has specific responsibilities they perform, such as making travel arrangements, driving the van, setting up, packing up, individual practice, managing their website, correspondence, and taking care of finances. The individual tasks of each group member make it possible for Ives to perform effectively on stage. Because they were performing almost every day, each member of the group had to stay focused for the greater good of the group. Each member had to do his part.

Try IT!

Read Romans 12:3-6.
What does it say that God has given to each member of the body of Christ?

_____

_____

Does this passage seem to say that God has given each person a particular gift? Why or why not?

_____

_____

_____

_____

_____

God makes his body healthy by gifting people like you and me and giving us a special job to do. Paul tells us in 1 Corinthians 14:5 that we should use our spiritual gifts "… so that the church may be edified." The word edify literally means to build up or construct. Paul says a few verses later in 1 Corinthians 14:12, "Since you are eager to have spiritual gifts, try to excel in gifts that build up the church." God gives spiritual gifts to his church so that the body can build itself up, withstand attacks from the enemy, and ultimately go forth in victory.

My wife has gifts of mercy and encouragement. God has gifted her so that she likes spending lots of time with wounded people. She listens and relates to them, but also offers wise counsel (gift of encouragement/counseling). Many lives have been transformed by God through her ministry. She also has the gift of mercy, so she feels the pain of other people. God has not given me those gifts. My gifts are leadership and knowledge. I like charting the way and studying the road map. When I'm doing what God has called me to do, others are built up and encouraged.

As you study this book, you will be challenged to determine what your spiritual gifts are. God will use you to build up others in his church through the good management of the gifts he's given you.

Try IT!

Read 1 Corinthians 13.
Notice that this chapter is squeezed in-between chapters 12 and 14.

_____

_____

Why is love so central to the operation of the gifts of the Spirit?

_____

_____

_____

_____

_____

The Organic Church

Just because a building has a sign on it that says, "church" doesn't mean it's a part of Christ's living organic body. Some churches are lifeless. The living, pulsating power of Jesus doesn't flow through them. Other churches are alive. It's easy to see the vision and watch each member show love for each other. Everybody is involved and feels important. There's a vibrant life flowing when you walk through the doors. I think of one such church that never ceases to amaze me by the Christ-likeness I see when I visit. Whenever I speak or fellowship in that church, I sense that the members are supernaturally placed there and that they really enjoy what they're doing. God's presence fills the services. I go away encouraged.

Try IT!

Think of an experience when you were in a church that felt alive? How did you feel?

_____

_____

How did you notice the various gifts of the Spirit functioning?

_____

_____

_____

_____

_____

Scripture refers to the church as the body of Christ, family of God, people of God, or temple of the Holy Spirit. One of the key differences between a living organic church and a lifeless one is the use of the gifts of the Spirit among the members.

When Christ is guiding his church, the gifts of the Spirit flow through each member, and the body functions organically. The gifts of the Spirit join the various parts of the body into a unified whole.

Finding Your Role

You don't become a father by reading a book and going to seminars. A man becomes a father by having children. When Sarah was born on September 16, 1991, I was thrust into the world of parenthood. Studying the subject before September 16, 1991 was helpful, but I jumped in with both feet after that date. Suddenly, all the reading material had a very clear, practical application. I was eager to learn because I had a real child to take care of.

Do IT!

Ask your pastor how you can most effectively use your particular gift(s) so that your church might be built up.

Many people attend church, learn about Christianity, or even participate in a church program. Yet, it doesn't mean as much because there's not a practical, personal application. When you start utilizing your God-given gift(s), a new world opens up to you. You'll notice that you're truly helping others, and it won't be a burden on you. In fact, you'll long to help others. It will come naturally, and be satisfying.

You will also feel a new responsibility to use your gift(s). The apostle Peter says, "Each one should use whatever gift he has received to serve others, faithfully administering God's grace in its various forms" (1 Peter 4:10). Without you, the body just won't function properly. You are very important in Christ's church.

When I get tired and weary in the Christian life, I often remember that Jesus is coming soon. And when he does come, I long to hear him say to me, "Well done, you good and faithful servant."

Remember IT!

What scripture verse stood out to you in this lesson?

_____

_____

_____

_____

_____

Main points:

1. Each member of Christ's church has a gift and plays a vital role in the church's health.
2. At least one gift is given to each believer.
3. 1 Corinthians 12, 14, Romans 12:3–8, Ephesians 4:7–13, and 1 Peter 4:7–11 are the main passages on gifts.

Apply IT!

1. Reread the gift passages, meditating about what gifts you have received.
2. Determine to use your gift, knowing that you and the body of Christ will be strengthened.
3. Encourage someone who is using his or her gift, telling that person how much you've benefited from his or her ministry.

What the Gifts Are Not

J obs were scarce and John was ready to give up and join the unemployment line. He noticed a zoo on the way home and walked in unannounced. The manager said that no jobs were available, so John turned to walk away.

The zoo manager stopped him and asked if he would be willing to wear a gorilla costume and substitute for the gorilla that had recently died. John agreed and enjoyed convincing the onlookers that he was a gorilla. He grunted and swung through the trees with reckless abandon.

On the second day, he swung from a rope and accidentally fell into the lion's pit. The lion licked his chops and walked toward John. John froze in fear. His thoughts were, "Do I yell and give away my identity or do I do nothing and risk my life?" He yelled. The lion shot back, "Shut up, or both of us will lose our jobs!"

Appearances can be deceiving. It's often hard to separate fact from fiction. Many, for example, believe that spiritual gifts are the same as natural talents. Others confuse spiritual gifts with Christian responsibilities, personality, or the fruit of the Spirit. Sometimes it helps to discover what something is by determining what it's not.

Natural Talents

Joe was brought up in a home where being a car mechanic was a way of life. He and his dad were always fiddling with engines. Joe felt confident in fixing cars. He had a "talent" to fix engines. People came to Joe for advice and help. This made Joe feel very special. He even became a mechanic. Yet, Joe was an agnostic. His parents were religious only in name, and Joe never had time or interest in religion.

Joe didn't have the gift of fixing cars because he was not a believer. He had a talent, rather, for mechanics that he developed over time.

All people have natural talents, regardless of whether or not they are filled with the Spirit. The gifts of the Spirit, however, are Spirit-endowed abilities that God gives to believers to build up his body, the church. God uses these God-given abilities to strengthen and extend his church throughout the world.

Some have tried to connect natural talents with spiritual gifts, but it's nearly impossible to connect the two. Gary Bugbee, an expert on spiritual gifts, says: "After personally leading over thirty thousand people through this discovery [gift] process, I have not been able to identify when, and for whom, a natural talent will be equivalent to a spiritual gift. In fact, many times there is no correlation between natural talents and spiritual gifts."[1] If someone who has interviewed 30,000 people about the gifts of the Spirit can't figure it out, neither can we.

Try IT!

Read Matthew 25:14-30.
What is Jesus' main point in the passage?

_____

_____

_____

How do these verses inspire you to use your spiritual gifts here and now (see 1 Peter 4:7-11)?

_____

_____

_____

_____

[1] Gary Bugbee, *What You Do Best in the Body of Christ,* (Grand Rapids, MI: Zondervan, 2005), p.53.

Now it is true that your spiritual gift of teaching might correspond with your secular employment of teaching high school math. On the other hand, you might have an entirely different spiritual gift, such as mercy, which doesn't necessarily apply to teaching mathematics at the local high school. Granted, your spiritual gift of mercy will give you supernatural patience with students who don't easily grasp math equations!

God determines who gets what gifts and his decision is completely his--100% sovereign. He doesn't consult anyone about his choice. He just does it.

Fruit of the Spirit

Have you ever been around a person that you didn't know, and yet you could immediately sense that he or she was a Christian? I've felt this sensation so strongly at times that I've simply said, "Are you a believer in Jesus?" Usually the response is yes.

What is it that makes a believer stand out? It's the manifestation of the fruit of the Spirit. Paul says in Galatians 5:22–23, "But the fruit of the Spirit is love, joy, peace, patience, kindness, goodness, faithfulness, gentleness and self-control. Against such things there is no law."

When the Spirit dwells in a person, that person will start manifesting the characteristics described as the "fruit of the Spirit." The Spirit works to transform Christians so that they have the depth of character the Bible talks about. It's not automatic or sudden. We are always "under construction."

Paul says a few verses earlier in Galatians 5: 16–18, "So I say, live by the Spirit, and you will not gratify the desires of the sinful nature. For the sinful nature desires what is contrary to the Spirit, and the Spirit what is contrary to the sinful nature. They are in conflict with each other, so that you do not do what you want. But if you are led by the Spirit, you are not under law"

Try IT!

Read Colossians 3:12-16 and Galatians 5:22-23.
Compare the fruit talked about in both places.

_____

_____

_____

What fruit is missing in your own life?

_____

_____

_____

_____

As we live in the Spirit, asking the Holy Spirit to fill us on a daily basis, he will produce the fruit of the Spirit in our lives. While all believers should manifest the same fruit of the Spirit, the spiritual gifts are distinct and sovereignly distributed. God determines which spiritual gifts go to each person. The fruit of the Spirit, on the other hand, is distributed to all equally. The Spirit's love, joy, peace, etc. should be manifested in the life of every believer.

The gifts of the Spirit foretell what function we'll play in the body of Christ and help us to know how we are called to minister in the cell, the local church, and even in the worldwide church of Jesus Christ. The fruit of the Spirit is the common language that all believers share.

Do IT!

Determine which fruit you lack the most and ask the Holy Spirit to abundantly develop that fruit in your life.

Christian Responsibilities

Whenever I'm at a Billy Graham crusade, I'm amazed at the simplicity with which he speaks. Because the Holy Spirit's anointing resides on him, when he gives the altar call, multitudes have responded and given their lives to Jesus. Billy Graham has the gift of evangelism. I don't have that gift. Yet, the Bible does tell me in numerous places that I need to share the Good News of Jesus Christ with those who don't know him.

My friend Jeff loves to help people. He looks for ways to serve others. I don't have the gift of helps like Jeff, but I'm still called to help others.

Christian responsibilities should never be avoided because we don't have such and such a gift. I've known some pastors who have stopped talking about the gifts of the Spirit because people were using the gifts as an excuse not to obey clear teaching of scripture. They would say, "I don't have the gift of mercy, so I'm not going to feed hungry people in the city." Or "I don't have the gift of teaching, so I'm not going to volunteer to teach children's church or to lead a cell group.

Try IT!

Read Romans 12:9-12 (notice that these verses are listed right after the spiritual gifts in verses 3-8).
What are the Christian responsibilities that Paul lists here?

_____

_____

_____

Which one(s) do you need to practice in your own life?

_____

_____

_____

You might not have the gift of giving, but God wants you to give generously. You might not have the gift of leadership, but God calls you to influence others for Christ. You might not have the gift of healing, but God still wants you to pray for people who are sick and hurting.

Personality Types

Some people get energy from interacting with people while others get their energy from spending time alone. Some make decisions based on their feelings while others stick with the facts. There is no right or wrong personality type. God made us all different.

I know there's a wide range of personality tests on the market, but I'm most familiar with the DISC personality test, which divides human personalities into four categories:

- D: driver (decisive, independent, efficient, practical, determined)
- I: inspiration (stimulating, enthusiastic, dramatic, outgoing, personable)
- S: steady (supportive, willing, dependable, reliable, agreeable)
- C: conscientious (thorough, persistent, orderly, serious, industrious)

Try IT!

What kind of personality do you have?

_____

What are the strengths and weaknesses of your personality type?

_____

_____

_____

_____

I like the categories in DISC because they are simple, clear, and usually right on. My wife, for example, is primarily a steady personality and I primarily have a driver personality. Knowing our personalities helps us relate to each other more effectively.

Spiritual gifts are distinct from personality types. God doesn't give the gift of teaching, for example, only to those who are extroverted, inspirational types (I've sat under my fair share of God-anointed teachers who were introverted). He might, in fact, choose to give the gift of evangelism to a shy, introverted person. God loves variety—just look at the rest of his creation. Be open to whatever gift God decides to give you. Don't limit the types of gifts to your own personality type.

Try IT!

Read Matthew 7:21-23.
What do these verses say about counterfeit gifts?

_____

_____

_____

_____

How can you avoid the error of verses 21-23?

_____

_____

_____

_____

_____

_____

Remember IT!

What was the main thing you learned from this lesson?

_____

_____

_____

_____

_____

Main points:

1. All believers should manifest the same fruit of the Spirit, listed in Galatians 5:22–23. God, however, chooses, the particular gifts that are given to each believer.
2. All Christians have a responsibility to obey the teaching of scripture, regardless of their specific gifts.
3. Each person has a distinct personality. The gifts of the Spirit don't necessarily match personality types.

Apply IT!

1. Determine the talents God has given you. How do they differ from your spiritual gifts?
2. Ask the Holy Spirit to produce the fruit of the Spirit in your life.
3. Ask the Holy Spirit to reveal areas of Christian responsibility in which you have failed to be obedient because you didn't feel "gifted."

The Gifts of Service

James, one of the leaders I've coached over the years, is an incredible servant. He would willingly volunteer to arrange travel, crunch numbers, or give me a ride. When I asked him to do things, I initially thought I was over-stepping, and that eventually he'd burn out and maybe even feel resentful. But as I mentored James over the years, I realized that his desire to help only grew stronger and stronger.

I began to understand that serving and helping others was the true desire of James. I was witnessing first-hand a person with the gift of helps and service who had no greater joy than to serve others. It dawned on me that if I didn't give James the opportunity to minister, he'd feel sidelined and neglected.

I've observed multiple people like James in Christ's church. I believe that God has blessed his church with gifts of service. These gifts provide needed assistance to strengthen his people, the body of Christ.

Try IT!

Read 1 Corinthians 12:7-11; 28-31, Ephesians 4: 7-11, and Romans 12:3-8. How many gifts are listed in these verses and what are their names?

_____

Were there any gifts on this list that were new to you?

_____

_____

No specific category like service gifts exist in the Bible. Rather it's just a way of organizing similar gifts under one heading. The gifts of service are found in Romans 12 and 1 Corinthians 12.

SERVICE GIFTS	KEY WORDS	DESIRES	SERVES BY
Helps (1 Cor. 12:28)	Assisting	Free others to use gifts	Helping
Service (Romans 12:7)	Meets needs	Help however and wherever	Practical support
Admin-istration (1 Cor. 12:28)	Planner	Organization	Providing the details
Faith (1 Cor. 12:9)	God-given confidence	To step out	Unwavering conviction
Mercy (Romans 12:8)	Comforter	To show compassion	Kindness
Giving (Romans 12:8)	Liberally gives	To share resources	Sharing

Help!

The husband and wife of a family of six in our church recently went on a three-day cruise. When they asked Celyce, my wife, to help take care of their kids, she gladly accepted. For Celyce, helping out is not a burden, it's her gifting. She enjoys it. A person with the gift of helps is able to serve through using his or her talents and to bless others in the body of Christ.

The gift of helps is the ability to give practical assistance that will encourage other believers. Those with the gift of helps lighten the load of other believers (1 Corinthians 12:28).

Epaphroditus, mentioned in Philippians 2:25, is an example of someone with the gift of helps. He sought Paul out with the intention of ministering to his physical needs, so that Paul could more effectively carry out his apostolic role.

People like Epaphroditus are energized by helping others. Those without the gift of helps should still offer acts of kindness, but they will probably find it hard and draining. However, for someone with the gift of helps, it's energizing.

If you're leading a cell group or are part of the leadership team, try to find people with the gift of helps to make phone calls, visit other people, bring refreshments and generally help lighten your load.

How's Your Serve?

Repeatedly in small-group ministry, I hear of burdened leaders who feel as if they don't have enough time to fulfill all the responsibilities of small-group leadership. When probing further, I often notice that these leaders haven't mobilized the giftedness of the people in their groups: it has become a one-man or one-woman show. In contrast, the best small-group leaders delegate frequently. These great leaders see their small groups come alive with gifted people who really want to be used.

The gift of service is the ability to identify unmet needs and to make use of available resources to meet those needs (Romans 12:7).

Try IT!

Read Romans 12:7 (service gift) and 1 Corinthians 12:28 (helps gift). Describe the gift of helps and service in your own words.

_____

_____

Do you believe that you have these two gifts? Why or why not?

_____

_____

_____

The service and the helps gifts are companion gifts. They chain together in people to create a double portion of desire to meet needs. Those with the gift of service never feel burdened when they're helping others. They long to help others. Christian Schwarz, researcher and author, discovered that 81% of people who had the gift of service also had the gift of helps, and that these two gifts were most frequently paired together.

Don't Overlook the Details

Jethro, the father-in-law of Moses, noticed that Moses was taking too much responsibility on himself. He realized that Moses would burn out under the strain, so he said, "What you are doing is not good. You and these people who come to you will only wear yourselves out. The work is too heavy for you; you cannot handle it alone" (Exodus 18:17–18). Jethro then recommended an organizational structure consisting of groups of tens, hundreds, and thousands. He suggested that Moses should only take on those cases that no one else could handle. Jethro had the gift of administration.

Try IT!

Read 1 Corinthians 12:28.
Name someone who you think has the gift of administration. Why do you believe he or she has this gift?

_____

_____

Is this a gift that God has given you? Why or why not?

_____

_____

_____

_____

The gift of administration is the God-given ability to plan and organize (1 Corinthians 12:28).

In the ancient Greek world, the word for administration was also translated as steering. The captain charted out the course, and the steersman followed the directions. A person with the gift of administration is able and ready to manage the work of God. He is able to serve in a special way. Those who like to organize activities might very well have this gift.

Those with the gift of administration don't have to organize events on a huge level. They might organize an event at the cell level, which is perfectly okay. In fact, I believe a person must start small and gradually work up to more responsibility.

Moving Mountains

Dan Brown's book, *90 Minutes in Heaven*, tells Dan's story of dying and going to heaven. Dan, a Southern Baptist pastor, met a semi-truck on a bridge that demolished his car and his body. The paramedics covered him with the white cloth because he was dead.

In the meantime a friend, Dick Onerecker, who at one time was a medic in Vietnam, saw the car, not knowing it was Dan's, and felt a strong compulsion to go and pray for the victim. The police tried to convince Dick of the utter futility in praying for a dead man, but Dick insisted. He crawled inside the mangled car and put his hand on the man's lifeless head and began to pray and sing.

Dan, who was enjoying the incredible bliss of heaven, suddenly felt a call to come back into his body. The rest of the book highlights the incredible struggles Dan faced as he tried to survive in his torn, broken body. After numerous difficult operations and painful surgeries, Dan is a walking testimony to God's grace and power.

I've given this book on various occasions to unbelievers because it's such a powerful testimony of the reality of heaven. The book also highlights Dick Onerecker's gift of faith. God has given a measure of faith to every believer, but God has blessed some with more faith than others.

The gift of faith is the ability to recognize what God wants to do in an impossible situation and then to trust God to get that task accomplished (1 Corinthians 12:9).

Someone with the gift of faith is able to see God-sized possibilities in the midst of trials and struggles. Such a person is able to press ahead in the face of major obstacles and not be discouraged even when very tough circumstances would dictate otherwise.

Jesus said in Mark 11:23, "I tell you the truth, if anyone says to this mountain, 'Go, throw yourself into the sea,' and does not doubt in his heart but believes that what he says will happen, it will be done for him." Those with the gift of faith are able to believe God for the impossible.

Try IT!

Read 1 Corinthians 12:9.
Describe the gift of faith in your own words?

_____

_____

Do you have this gift? Why or why not?

_____

_____

_____

_____

_____

_____

Have Mercy

When you live with someone for twenty years, you get to know that person quite well. As I've observed my wife Celyce over these past twenty years, I've noticed three crystal clear gifts in her: helps, counseling, and mercy.

Recently her dad, Leo, was admitted to a nursing home because of his Parkinson's disease. Even though my wife drives two hours each way to visit him, she's there each week. Celyce is attracted to those in need (I'm sure I'll be blessed in my older age!). Her mercy gift was probably the underlying reason she earned her BA in nursing and went into that practice before we left for Ecuador in 1990.

Those with the gift of mercy feel the pain of others. They empathize with people in pain and easily put themselves into the sufferer's place.

The mercy gift is a God-given supernatural compassion for neglected people (Romans 12:8).

Try IT!

Read what Romans 12:8 says about the gift of mercy.
Name a person who has the gift of mercy. How does this person act?

_____

_____

_____

Do you believe you have this gift? Why or why not?

_____

_____

_____

_____

_____

Those with this gift don't simply offer words of encouragement; they give practical aid to people who are troubled in mind, body, or spirit. People with the gift of mercy will often have a ministry to the handicapped, the elderly, the mentally disabled or drug addicts.

Members of the cell group who have this gift will often make suggestions for outreach to the poor and help for the needy. Since Jesus himself was so concerned about meeting such needs, he energizes his church to do the same.

Do IT!
Reflect on each of the gifts listed in this lesson and determine if God has given you one of these gifts.

Give Generously

Robert attends one of our cell groups. On several occasions he's insisted on taking the entire cell out to dinner (on a couple occasions he spent more than $90.00 at a fast-food restaurant!). Robert just loves to give, give, and give some more—whether it's food, money, or Christian love. On at least two occasions, when church families were moving, he personally paid for large moving vans so that the move could be done quickly and effeciently. Robert runs his own business, and he practices that same generous giving with his clients. His generosity is one of the main reasons why his business is growing and prospering.

The giving gift is the ability to share money and other possessions both generously and cheerfully (Romans 12:8).

People with this gift usually give significantly beyond the normal tithe, sometimes most of their income. Those with the gift of giving freely share their gifts with those in the body of Christ and even outside the body of Christ.

The gift of giving is a wonderful gift that God uses in his body to bless his people. Since ministry is not primarily a money-making endeavor, those with the gift of giving are used by God to bless God's people from a practical, material standpoint.

Memorize IT!
"Each one should use whatever gift he has received to serve others, faithfully administering God's grace in its various forms" (1 Peter 4:10).

Remember IT!

What truth stood out to you in this lesson?

_____

_____

_____

_____

_____

_____

_____

Main points:

1. The service gifts include: helps, service, administration, faith, mercy, and giving.
2. The purpose of the service gifts are to build up Christ's body through acts of service.
3. Those gifted with one of the service gifts find joy in helping others.

Apply IT!

1. Meditate on each passage listed in this lesson.
2. Determine if God has given you one of the service gifts.
3. Find ways to use that service gift in the cell, worship service, and in your daily life.

The Gifts of Equipping

I consider Dave Coopersmith an equipper. As a friend, he knew I needed help in my house in Moreno Valley. When we first moved in 2001 to our home, I struggled with fixing a faucet, replacing the string on the weed-eater, or replacing a door hinge. Dave graciously fixed those items for me, while he explained to me what he was doing. The next time the problem happened, Dave asked me to fix it while he watched. He guided me to do a better job, but he didn't do it for me. With new confidence I was willing to even try to fix things on my own, now I'm far more confident to fix things around the house.

It wasn't long before Dave was equipping my daughter Sarah to play piano and my daughter Nicole to play guitar. Dave would show them what he knew on both piano and guitar, but he didn't stop there. He had them play. It wasn't long before Dave invited my daughters to play on the worship team at our church. Dave finds joy in equipping others for ministry.

God has raised up gifted men and women to equip others to do the work of the ministry. Ephesians 4:11–13 says, "It was he who gave some to be apostles, some to be prophets, some to be evangelists, and some to be pastors and teachers, to prepare [equip] God's people for works of service, so that the body of Christ may be built up."

Those who God has gifted to equip his church find joy in extending their own ministries through others. They desire to raise up a multitude of workers who continue the process. What is the reason for this? Paul tells us in Ephesians 4:13–14 that "until we all reach unity in the faith and in the knowledge of the Son of God and become mature, attaining to the whole measure of the fullness of Christ. Then we will no longer be infants, tossed back and forth by the waves, and blown here and there by every wind of teaching and by the cunning and craftiness of men in their deceitful scheming."

Those gifts that I have placed in the equipping category are found in Ephesians 4, Romans 12, and Corinthians 12.

EQUIPPING GIFTS	KEY WORDS	DESIRES	LEADS BY
Pastoring (Eph. 4:11)	Shepherd	To care for/ protect	Sensitivity to people
Leadership (Rom. 12:8)	Orchestrator	To give direction	Vision/Goals Inspiration/
Exhortation (Rom. 12:8)	Encourager	To motivate	Practical application
Evangelism (Eph. 4:11)	Evangelist	New Christians	Burden for unsaved
Apostle (1 Cor. 12:8)	Foundation builder	New churches	God-given authority
Teaching (1 Cor. 12:28)	Doctrine developer	To teach	Biblical obedience
Knowledge (1 Cor. 12:8)	Researcher for the body of Christ	Gathers knowledge and presents it	Sharing the facts
Wisdom (1 Cor. 12:8)	Understanding	To apply knowledge	God-given insight

Sheep Need Shepherds

I'm the lead pastor of a church in California, but I don't have the gift of pastoring. My associate pastor, Justin, does have the gift of pastoring. He loves to care for the sheep and make sure they are cared for and discipled.

Pastoring is the caring for and feeding a group of believers. Those with the gift of pastoring protect the group under their care from error (Ephesians 4:11).

Paul exhorted the shepherds at Ephesus to "Keep watch over yourselves and all the flock of which the Holy Spirit has made you overseers. Be shepherds of the church of God, which he bought with his own blood" (Acts 20:28).

The official full-time pastor of the church might not have the gift of pastoring. The person who does have this gift might work at a computer company. Often the pastor of the local church will have the gift of leadership or teaching. Some pastors have the gift of evangelism and delegate the day to day pastoral responsibilities to others.

Someone with the gift of pastoring might be a volunteer member of a small group or leading one. Those with this gift make sure God's flock is well taken care of. They are concerned with the health of the flock. Those with the gift of pastoring are also very concerned with protecting God's sheep from enemy attack. They want to make sure the sheep are well-fed, and that they don't go astray.

Try IT!

Read Ephesians 4:11.
Name someone who you believe has the gift of pastoring. Why do you believe he or she has this gift?

_____

_____

_____

Do you believe that you have the gift of pastoring? Why or why not?

_____

_____

_____

_____

I Will Follow

In one sense we are all called to influence others. A father and mother influence their sons and daughters. A wise teacher inspires students. A good-hearted employer influences the workers to give 100%.

We are all called to influence others, but those with the gift of leadership have a special, supernatural capacity to stimulate others to a greater vision than they have. Then they stir people forward to reach their goals.

The leadership gift is the ability to influence and inspire people to expect great things from God and attempt great things for God (Romans 12:8).

Try IT!

Read what Romans 12:8 says about the gift of leadership.
Describe the gift of leadership in your own words.

_____

_____

_____

Do you feel that God has given you the gift of leadership? Why or why not?

_____

_____

_____

_____

_____

_____

_____

I don't believe that a cell leader needs to have the gift of leadership to effectively lead a cell.[1] But those with the gift of leadership are often those who lead networks of cell groups, serve as elders in the church, or pastor the church.

Nor do I believe that a person with the gift of leadership necessarily will be the pastor or visible leader in a church. Often those with the gift of leadership work behind the scenes, influencing and inspiring others by their faithful example. Yet, when key decisions need to be made, everyone wants to know what so-and-so thinks. Why? Because he or she has the gift of leadership.

Counsel Me

Laura, a cell leader, is very quiet and doesn't like to speak in front of groups. But she comes alive in one-on-one counseling sessions. Often after the cell group, Laura will connect to those who are having problems, establish a relationship with the person, and then maintain a counseling relationship.

This gift of counseling is actually called "exhortation" in the Bible. It's the ability to come alongside someone to comfort and counsel (Romans 12:8). Those who have studied the gifts of the Spirit frequently refer to this gift as the counseling gift.

All people need some form of counsel. Even those who outwardly smile and seem optimistic crash and burn. Perhaps what has driven them is a need for attention. And those with the gift of counseling are able to offer that word that pierces through the disappointments and directs the person to the living God, where he or she can sit and listen to God in a new, fresh way.

The cell group meeting is a great place to give general counseling, yet much of the best counseling takes place before or after the actual cell meeting. Those with the exhortation gift often linger in order to listen, bear the burdens of others, and offer choice advice that ministers to those with needs.

---

[1] My twenty-nine question survey distributed to 700 cell leaders in eight countries showed that the leader's gift did not affect group multiplication. After all, the effective leaders utilize all the gifts within the cell group.

Try IT!

Read what Romans 12:8 says about the gift of exhortation
Many consider this gift to be associated with counseling. Name a person who demonstrates this gift in his or her life.

_____

_____

_____

Do you feel that you have the gift of exhortation? Why or why not?

_____

_____

_____

Spreading the Good News

Whenever I speak to my friend, Gary, he's always talking about evangelism. He breathes evangelism. When new people aren't receiving Christ, Gary saddens. Gary is also very effective at evangelism, and I'm constantly confirming Gary's evangelism gift. Such affirmation simply encourages Gary to do what he's good at.

The evangelism gift is the ability to effectively communicate the gospel to non-believers and lead them to Jesus (Ephesians 4:11).

Everyone is called to evangelize, but those with the gift of evangelism will have added desire to evangelize and fruit to show for it. People with the gift of evangelism exude vision to reach non-believers and find it quite annoying when believers are more interested in perfecting themselves than going out to the highways and byways to preach the gospel to unbelievers. Those with the gift of evangelism find it easy to talk to unbelievers—more natural than talking with Christians.

Try IT!

Read what Ephesians 4:11 says about the gift of evangelism.
Billy Graham is associated with this gift, but how would you describe how a person could use this gift in everyday life?

_____

_____

_____

Do you believe that you have the gift of evangelism? Why or why not?

_____

_____

_____

Starting Churches

The most famous example of an apostle in scripture is Paul. You can hardly mention Paul's name without adding the title apostle. Paul launched out on three missionary tours and planted churches throughout the Roman Empire during the first century. Paul would start the church plants and then turn them over to his co-workers, while he continued planting more churches.

The origins of the Greek word *apostle* refer to an admiral over a fleet of ships, which, under orders from a ruler, would start a colony. Paul the apostle was under orders from Jesus Christ to plant a colony of churches throughout the Mediterranean region.

The person with the apostleship gift is normally recognized as a spiritual leader by a variety of churches (1 Corinthians 12:28).

The gift of apostleship is alive and well in the church today and desperately needed as the population rate continues to soar, and more and more people need a church nearby.

Are apostles confined to church planters? I believe that non-church planters can also be apostles—but in another sense. Those who strongly influence church planters and Christian workers through writing and spiritual leadership might also be considered apostles.

Teaching the Faithful

Have you noticed the difference between speakers who clearly articulate a Bible passage so that you go away saying, "Wow I've never heard those Bible verses explained in such an easy-to-understand way." Most likely the person you were hearing has the gift of teaching.

Those with the gift of teaching love to study the Bible and can't find enough time to pour over the Scriptures. Their personal Bible study comes out when they teach God's word. They bring out details of Scriptures that others didn't even know existed.

The gift of teaching allows a person to clarify and simplify God's word (1 Corinthians 12:28).

Great teachers focus on the questions of their listeners, rather than expounding on theory after theory that only has relevance to the teacher. And someone with the gift of teaching doesn't need to preach to exercise their gift. A cell member, for example, might have the gift of teaching. He or she is able to clarify scripture in such an articulate way that others are encouraged grow in their Christian lives. Those with the gift of teaching are able to clarify difficult verses in a way that is simple and meaningful to those who hear.

One of the best ways to use the gift of teaching is to study the Bible and then make up questions for others to answer. Fred, for example, diligently prepared all week for his Thursday night group. I fully expected a Bible study, complete with exegesis, opinions from commentators, and illustrations. To my astonishment, Fred spoke very little that night. He skillfully drew the information from us. Although he had scrutinized the Bible passage, he led us to dig up the treasures for ourselves. He peppered us with questions that forced us to delve deeper and deeper into the text. Fred had the gift of teaching, but he empowered others to discover God's Word for themselves.

Try IT!

Read what 1 Corinthians 12:28 says about the gift of teaching.
As you think of people who have taught you, does one or two stand out as
truly having the gift of teaching? What made that person unique?

_____

_____

_____

Has God given you the gift of teaching? Why or why not?

_____

_____

_____

_____

I Need to Know

Some view the gift of knowledge as supernatural insight that God drops upon a person to declare future events. You might have heard someone on TV saying something like, "I'm hearing God tell me that there's someone with a back injury that needs prayer right now." I wholeheartedly believe that God gives supernatural insight to a person. God has spoken to me through such "words" on several occasions. I would define, however, that phenomenon as the gift of prophecy.

A person with the gift of knowledge, on the other hand, has the ability to collect and analyze knowledge from a wide variety of sources, and then to apply that knowledge through writing, teaching, and preaching (1 Corinthians 12:8).

Often those with the gift of knowledge are able to write and gather facts that help others. I have this gift. I love to piece facts together and then place those facts into book form where others can readily assimilate those facts and use them for their own ministries.

Most likely Luke had this gift, as did Solomon, who wrote the book of Proverbs and labored long and hard to write down so many truths.

Do IT!
Name someone you know with an equipping gift. Encourage that person by either writing a note of thanks or personally talking with the person. Share how you've benefited from his or her ministry.

Wisdom from Above

My older brother, Jay Comiskey, has the gift of wisdom. Whenever I'm in a tight spot and need wisdom on how to answer a person or take the next step in ministry, I go to Jay for advice. Jay has the ability to paint the whole picture and then to offer specific advice. Others have also noticed Jay's gift of wisdom. In the 70s Jay hitch-hiked from California to Virginia and began working in the stockroom at the Christian Broadcasting Network. Now Jay is one of the vice-presidents at CBN. Jay has repeatedly demonstrated the ability to make wise decisions in stressful situations.

The wisdom gift includes the ability to apply God's wisdom to various situations (1 Corinthians 12:8).

It's one thing to possess knowledge; it's quite another to know what to do with the knowledge. Those with the gift of wisdom are able to understand God's plan and then help people to grapple with the implication of their decisions. The gift of wisdom often manifests itself over time. Others begin to recognize the consistent, solid advice that those with the gift of wisdom give.

Memorize IT!
"Therefore, I urge you, brothers, in view of God's mercy, to offer your bodies as living sacrifices, holy and pleasing to God---this is your spiritual act of worship" (Romans 12:1).

Remember IT!

What truth in this lesson stood out to you the most?

_____

_____

_____

_____

_____

_____

_____

Main points:

1. The equipping gifts help members of Christ's church by preparing them to do God's work more effectively and, therefore, build up and empower the church.
2. The equipping gifts listed in this lesson include pastoring, leadership, exhortation, evangelism, apostleship, teaching, knowledge, and wisdom.
3. Those with the equipping gifts find joy in extending their own ministry through others.

Apply IT!

1. Determine whether God has given you one of the equipping gifts listed in this lesson.
2. Encourage those who are currently equipping you. Give them a word of encouragement or contribute financially to their ministry.
3. If you've been given one of the equipping gifts, think of specific ways that you can exercise that gift in the small group, the worship service, or in daily life.

The Gifts of Prayer and Worship

I remember when Harold Weitz asked Celyce and me to come forward in front of a thousand member crowd at a conference in South Africa in 1999. We knew that Pastor Harold was well-known for his prophetic gifts, but we weren't expecting to receive a prophecy before that many people. His prophecy for us lasted almost five minutes! One small part of the word was this: "Now, know this today, this is the hour, says God, that you will go forth, and a new mantle falls on this night for you; this is your experience of the burning bush that you've waited for; this is the experience, says the Lord, for from this night, I will cause you not to rest, and you will move endlessly and tirelessly. As my servant Paul, says the Lord, the same kind of anointing will rest on your life."

Immediately after he prophesied over us, I preached, just as I had done each of the previous three nights. But something was very different this time. I saw Jesus in a new way. I felt his control and power. It was no longer Joel Comiskey standing up to preach after practicing incessantly for hours. My burdens lifted. Jesus became so real that night that I felt like I could touch him—just like he had been so real when he first touched me and healed me in 1973. My words flowed effortlessly. I was no longer trying to impress the group, but simply allowing Jesus to flow through me. It was his work, not my own.

I bought the tape and wrote down every word of Harold's prophecy. I still reread it on occasion when I need encouragement. And this is the purpose of prophecy—encouragement, joy and strength. 1 Corinthians 14:3 says, "But everyone who prophesies speaks to men for their strengthening, encouragement and comfort."

That night in South Africa, God supernaturally showed me that he's alive and well. God uses the prayer and worship gifts to remind people that he's just as alive today as when he appeared to his disciples after his resurrection. Hebrews 13:8 declares, "Jesus Christ is the same yesterday and today and forever."

PRAYER/ WORSHIP GIFTS	KEY WORDS	DESIRES	SERVES BY
Miracles (1 Cor. 12:10)	Mountain mover	To manifest God's power	Supernatural signs
Prophecy (1 Cor. 12:10)	Speak forth authority	Proclaim truth	Scripture
Tongues (1 Cor. 12:10)	Unknown words	Ministry of worship to God, personal edification	Another language
Interpretation of tongues (1 Cor. 12:10)	Tongue's mouthpiece	Edify church	Interpreting
Healings (1 Cor. 12:9)	Healings	To manifest God's power	Supernatural healings
Discernment of Spirits (1 Cor. 12:10)	Spiritual pulse	Distinguish good from evil	Spiritual analysis

I Need a Miracle

As a young Christian, I attended the famous Calvary Chapel of Costa Mesa, CA where the Jesus Movement started. I devoured Chuck Smith's teaching, and one of the aspects I loved about Chuck's teaching was that he didn't deny that God's miracles were for today. Rather, he taught that Jesus Christ was just as alive and present today as when he rose again.

The Bible is not an end in itself. Rather, it is God's inspired word that points to the God of miracles. And he still loves to do miracles today.

The gift of miracles is the ability to believe God for mighty acts that are contrary to the laws of nature and that glorify God for the miraculous events (1 Corinthians 12:10).

Miracles are supernatural gifts that God gives to certain members of his body that allows the person to do supernatural things. God still does miracles today. He's the same yesterday today and forever. He never changes. And because he never changes, we should expect to see great things take place among us. Those with the gift of miracles can pray for unusual happenings and see God answer in a mighty way. They are able to believe God for what seems impossible and then trust God to keep his promise.

God Speaks Today

In the film, *Facing the Giants*, one of the characters feels an impression from God to go to the discouraged coach and say, "Coach, God is not through with you yet." This coach, on the verge of being fired, was renewed with energy and vigor. He was inspired to press ahead. And prophesy is meant to do exactly that—inspire a God-greatness in us.

Only God can work in a mighty way and manifest himself. Prophesy inspires God's people to think outside the box and believe God for the impossible. Prophesy gives great comfort to know that God is actually alive and working among his people.

Prophecy is the ability to receive a message from God and then to speak it forth to his Church (1 Corinthians 12:10).

This is an important gift because the Holy Spirit uses it to manifest his presence, assuring people that he's alive and speaking directly to them.

Jehoshaphat, a king of Judah, had to face an enemy army that far outnumbered him. The odds were impossible. So he asked his people to fast, and they waited on God. As they waited and cried out to God, the Spirit of the LORD came upon Jahaziel, and he prophesied saying, "Listen, King Jehoshaphat and all who live in Judah and Jerusalem! This is what the LORD says to you: 'Do not be afraid or discouraged because of this vast army. For the battle is not yours, but God's. Tomorrow march down against them. You will not have to fight this battle. Take up your positions; stand firm and see the deliverance the LORD will give you, O Judah and Jerusalem. Do not be afraid; do not be discouraged. Go out to face them tomorrow, and the LORD will be with you'" (2 Chronicles 20:14–17). God gave Jehoshaphat and his people an incredible victory.

The misconception with prophesy is that it has to be a disruptive, future message that normally causes huge adjustments to the one receiving it. God doesn't normally deal with us in this way and rarely does prophesy work in this manner. The vast majority of time, prophesy assures people of God's love, grace, and plan for them. Prophesy helps people to see that God is working behind the scenes and does indeed have a perfect plan that he's unfolding in his time.

Try IT!

Read what 1 Corinthians 12:10 says about the gift of prophesy.
What has been your understanding of the gift of prophesy up to this point?

_____

_____

_____

How has your view changed since reading this lesson? Do you believe that you have this gift? Why or why not?

_____

_____

_____

_____

_____

_____

Prophetic abuse has happened and does happen, and many have been vaccinated against the real thing. I was in one church that has a prophetic Sunday school class, in which they invited anyone to come in and receive a prophetic word. Yet, the leader of this prophetic meeting told me that each prophesy had to squarely be in line with scripture and needed to positively build up the hearer. Knowing the dangers, they steered away from predictions about the future. I firmly believe that God gives prophesies about the future to his people. I also believe, however, that those offering such prophesies should have a mature and proven prophetic ministry.

Unknown Languages

Speaking in tongues is for today! This gift has not ceased. I know that many people have problems with this gift. On one hand, people hold it up as THE gift that accompanies the filling of the Spirit. On the other hand, there are those who dismiss this gift and blackball everyone who believes in it.

The gift of the tongues is the ability to receive and to speak a divine utterance in a language unknown to the person (1 Corinthians 12:10).

The gift of tongues is primarily for the building up of the believer who speaks in an unknown language. It's a prayer language that stirs the believer to talk specifically to God and grow in his relationship with the Almighty. Many who have the gift of tongues use it in their personal prayer life. If God has given you the gift of tongues, the best place to use it is in your quiet time. Speaking in tongues is a great benefit in worship because often words can't express our torrent of desire. Often I'll speak in tongues in my quiet time because I know I'm ministering directly to the heart of God (1 Corinthians 14:2).

When using the gift of tongues in public, there should always be an interpreter (see 1 Corinthians 14:27–28). The Bible makes it clear that in public it's far better to speak in words that people understand rather than words that are unintelligible. Paul said in 1 Corinthians 14:18–19, "I thank God that I speak in tongues more than all of you. But in the church I would rather speak five intelligible words to instruct others than ten thousand words in a tongue."

Try IT!

Read what 1 Corinthians 12:10 says about tongues.
Describe the gift of tongues in your own words.

_____

_____

_____

Have you ever spoken in tongues? Why or why not?

_____

_____

_____

Would You Interpret That?

One church that I greatly admire makes it a practice to wait on the Lord before the preaching service to see if members want to prophesy or speak in tongues. I've heard various members speak in tongues, but each gift of tongue was followed by someone with the gift of interpretation. It was done decently and in order, just like it says in 1 Corinthians 14:33, "For God is not a God of disorder but of peace."

Those who interpret tongues have the ability to take a message communicated in tongues and make it known in a commonly understood language (1 Corinthians 12:10).

Often those who interpret also have been given the gift of tongues or prophecy. Sometimes the person who speaks in tongues interprets their own message. What's most important, however, is that someone does interpret the gift of tongues given in a public meeting.

In the small-group format, the leader should instruct those with the gift of tongues that the public gift of tongues always requires an interpretation. The leader might even want to tell the person with tongues to pray for interpretation or not to speak, but if the leader has this gift of interpretation, he or she should be ready to offer the interpretation.

Mistakes and failures do happen in small-group ministry—just like in every other aspect of life. Yet, without the liberty to experiment, there's the very real danger of limiting or putting out the Spirit's fire. While all the practices of spiritual gifts must be guided by God's inerrant word, let's remember that they should be practiced. In fact we are commanded to manage our gifts well (1 Peter 4:10).

Heal Me, Lord

In 1974, I joined a ministry called Shekinah, based out of Long Beach, California. As a brand new Christian, I was enthralled by the healing ministry at Shekinah. This ministry would send out teams of people to different churches throughout California to conduct healing services. I learned from my experience with Shekinah that I couldn't manipulate God's healing power. He healed those who he wanted to heal, and I couldn't force my will on his. I also discovered that I didn't have the particular gift of healing.

Others in Shekinah did have this gift, and God used them consistently to pray over people and see them healed. If you've prayed for people to be healed and seen powerful results, there's a good chance that you have this gift of healing.

The gift of healings is the ability to pray for healing and see results (1 Corinthians 12:9).

But healing is not only about praying for sick people. In 1 Corinthians 12:9, Paul uses the term gift of healings, which refers to healing in the emotional and spiritual realms as well.

Try IT!

Read about the gift of healings in 1 Corinthians 12:9.
Knowing that the gift of healings is more than just for physical healings, do you know someone who has this gift?

_____

_____

_____

Has God given you this gift? Why or why not?

_____

_____

_____

_____

So many physical problems have their roots in emotional brokenness. God sometimes heals a person physically, while at other times he works on the emotional state that caused the problem. God's special healing agents might be trained counselors, doctors, or ministers.

Do IT!

Go to someone who needs healing (physical, spiritual, or emotional) and pray for that person, expecting God to heal.

Bad Vibes

We have a woman in our cell who has the gift of discerning spirits. She is very sensitive to wickedness in the world and the church. She admits that at times it's very hard to manage this gift because she can quickly discern the presence of evil and she's forced to make clear stands against wickedness.

The gift of discernment helps a person distinguish between truth and error, and to know with certainty when a behavior is of satanic, human or divine origin (1 Corinthians 12:10).

Those with the gift of discernment are especially endowed with the ability to know with certainty what is true and what is false. Jesus said, "Watch out for false prophets. They come to you in sheep's clothing, but inwardly they are ferocious wolves" (Matthew 7:15).

The gift of discernment is multi-faceted and practical. It seems to be tied in with wisdom. If a person is struggling with personal issues and could be confused because of Satan's deception and lying, someone with the gift of discernment can speak truth into his or her life and guide the person down the right path.

Try IT!

Read 1 Corinthians 12:10 about the discernment of spirits. Describe the gift of discernment in your own words.

_____

_____

_____

Has God given you this gift? Why or why not?

_____

_____

_____

The gift of discernment of spirits can also be used on a personal level. It helps a person sort out the truth and error in their own lives and struggles.

Remember IT!

What stood out to you in this lesson?

_____

_____

_____

_____

_____

Main points:

1. The prayer and worship gifts include prophesy, tongues, interpretation of tongues, miracles, healings, and the discernment of spirits.
2. The prayer and worship gifts remind us that God is alive and working in our lives today.
3. God is ultimately sovereign over all, and he won't be manipulated by the prayer and worship gifts (e.g., everyone must be healed).

Apply IT!

1. Reread the prayer and worship gifts listed in this lesson.
2. Determine if God has given you one or more of the "prayer and worship gifts."
3. Practice using that gift in your cell, worship service, and daily life.

How Do I Discover My Spiritual Gifts?

Many of us have memorized the words, "In 1492, Columbus sailed the ocean blue." It's commonly thought that Christopher Columbus discovered the Americas at that time. Yet it wasn't until 1498, on his third voyage that Columbus reached the mainland. 1492 does have a lot of significance because Columbus set sail at that time and continued to explore until his last voyage in 1502. 1492 is an important year because Columbus launched his lifetime quest of discovery that revolutionized travel and exploration at that time.

It's interesting to note that in 1492, Columbus nearly failed when his crew threatened to commit mutiny against him. Yet, he didn't give up. He tried again and again. He continued exploring, improving his navigation skills over time. Eventually, he made astounding discoveries that changed the course of history.

Finding your spiritual gift is a challenging process of discovery that doesn't happen overnight. It's a process of stepping out, learning, and making mid-course adjustments.

Discovery Happens Best in an Intimate Environment

Over thirty-two years ago I first started exercising my leadership gift by guiding a cell group at my parent's house. I was only a few years old as a Christian and stumbled badly when I delivered my lesson. I remember when Bob Burtch, the worship leader in the group, took me aside after one of my rambling messages and said, "You really need to work on your delivery, Joel." Bob was a great friend and felt free to challenge me. I challenged him as well. Everyone in the group brought a song, a Scripture, or a testimony.

It's through God-ordained relationships that we grow together. And it's in this context that we learn how to grow in the Christian life. The small group is an ideal context to make that happen.

Try IT!

Read Acts 2:42-46 and 5:42.
Where did the early church meet?

_____

_____

Share how you have been able to use your gifts in the context of the cell group.

_____

_____

_____

_____

_____

Actually, the Biblical passages about the gifts of the Spirit were first written to house churches in the first century. In such a small group environment Paul could expect them to use their gifts and receive feedback. The same is true in the twenty-first century.

Experiment with Various Gifts

In the larger worship service, naturally experimenting with the gifts rarely happens because risk-taking is not encouraged in such an environment, nor should it be. Yet, in the safety of the small group and with the encouragement of the group leader, experimentation can happen, and the Holy Spirit will bless. When you're sitting in a comfortable living room with just a few people, there's far more possibilities to talk with and minister to others.

Once the group becomes comfortable with each other and more knowledgeable about spiritual gifts, the leader can encourage the participants to confirm in each other their spiritual gifts in the small-group time. Gift discovery takes place in the process of serving one another, caring for one another, and living the life of the body. When you find that God consistently blesses your efforts in a certain area that builds others up, you can confidently conclude that you have that particular gift.

Try IT!

Read 1 Corinthians 14: 26.
How should all of the gifts be exercised?

_____

_____

_____

_____

How do you plan to build up Christ's church through your gift?

_____

_____

_____

_____

_____

Some churches magnify just one or two gifts, to the exclusion of others. Some have called this process gift colonization. If the pastor is a gifted evangelist with regular campaigns, there may be a strong tendency to organize the entire church around evangelism. The other gifts of the Holy Spirit may be less likely to be manifested in the church because like-minded people will either stay or leave, depending on whether or not they like the pastor.

Great group facilitators, on the other hand, allow for more diversity. The leader needs to be open to allow people to experiment with gifts that are different from his or her own gifting—as long as the use of that gift edifies the rest of the group. As the leader gives members more liberty to exercise their gifts, the members will experience a new responsibility and will consequently feel more committed to the church.

What Do You Like to Do?

Some people scratch their head when they hear that I'm a writer. They can't believe that I could actually enjoy collecting and organizing facts and then writing them down in a book. This seems so foreign to them because it is not what they enjoy doing. But because I have the gift of knowledge, I get high on learning and writing my ideas down for a book. Someone else would be completely exhausted by writing, but would find immense pleasure in counseling, for example. It just depends on the gifting that God has given to you.

Normally when using your gift you'll go away saying, "Wow, I love doing this!" If you feel that you have the gift of teaching, the first question you should ask yourself is, "Do I like explaining biblical truth?" If you have the spiritual gift of healing, you need to ask, "Do I enjoy praying for people? Does God heal some of them?"

Perhaps you have the gift of helps and administration. The key questions are, "Do I love to bring refreshments? Do I love to organize events in the group?" If you have the gift of mercy, you'll want to ask, "Am I drawn to visit cell members who are having problems?"

Joy and excitement accompany the proper use of spiritual gifts. You most likely have a particular gift that, when you practice it, you experience inner joy, are filled with excitement and energy, and are fulfilled. When it feels heavy and burdensome to exercise a spiritual gift, it might be because no such gift is operating.

Try IT!

Read 1 Corinthians 14:1.
Describe Paul's counsel in your own words?

_____

_____

_____

What particular gifts do you eagerly desire? Why or why not?

_____

_____

_____

_____

_____

Seek Confirmation from Others

Timothy was the apostle Paul's spiritual son. Paul mentored Timothy and eventually left him in Ephesus to pastor. Timothy felt inadequate because of his youth, so Paul encouraged him saying, "Don't let anyone look down on you because you are young, but set an example for the believers in speech, in life, in love, in faith and in purity" (1 Timothy 4:12). On another occasion, Timothy was fearful about exercising his spiritual gift, so Paul said to him, "I remind you to fan into flame the gift of God, which is in you through the laying on of my hands. For God did not give us a spirit of timidity, but a spirit of power, of love and of self-discipline" (2 Timothy 1:7–8).

Timothy needed Paul's encouragement to press ahead in the face of obstacles. He also needed Paul's confirmation of the spiritual gifts he had already received—and the need to use them. We, like Timothy, need affirmation and confirmation of our spiritual gifts.

Try IT!

Has anyone ever confirmed a particular gift in your own life?

_____

_____

_____

If yes, describe the spiritual gift (s) and the situation when it was confirmed.

_____

_____

_____

What do people confirm in you? If they notice your capacity to clarify the meaning of Scripture, you may have the gift of teaching. The gifts were given to edify of the body of Christ, and when you build up someone with your gift, others will let you know. Once the group becomes comfortable with each other and more knowledgeable about spiritual gifts, ask someone else about what gift they think you have.

What if no one tells you? My advice is to ask someone you respect. Jesus said, "Ask and it will be given to you; seek and you will find; knock and the door will be opened to you. For everyone who asks receives; he who seeks finds; and to him who knocks, the door will be opened" (Matthew 7:7–8). Ask mature and godly people you know to confirm your spiritual gift. This will give you a better picture of your special place in the body of Christ.

Do IT!
Ask someone you respect about what gifts he or she thinks you have.

Spiritual gift tests can be helpful, and I've benefitted from taking such tests on various occasions (see Appendix 2). People can project, however, the gifts they'd like to have on such gift tests, so it is not a fool-proof way to discover your gifts. A much safer and more effective method is to experiment with various gifts around those who know and love you. Then ask for their feedback.

Using Your Gifts in Daily Life

Although the primary application of spiritual giftedness is found in the church, I believe the Spirit also wants us to use his gifts to reach a lost world. Our gifts can be used wherever we are—work, home, school—not just within the church.

Perhaps when you are talking with a friend or colleague at work, a particular need arises. The same Spirit who was at work in your small group the night before wants to use you right then and there. Ask the Spirit to give you wisdom and to manifest his gifts through you, whether they are helps, miracles, or the discernment of spirits.

If you have the gift of mercy, God might use you in hospital visitation, whether or not you're visiting a church member. Those with the gift of evangelism will take their gift wherever they are. Dr. Robert L. Saucy, professor at Talbot Seminary, says, "Since the church is the church whether members are gathered for corporate meeting or scattered in their homes and communities, the ministry of gifts can take place in all situations."[1]

---

[1] As quoted in *Are Miraculous Gifts for Today?* Editor Wayne Grudem (Grand Rapids, MI.: Zondervan, 1996), p. 141.

Try IT!

How can you use your spiritual gift(s) at home, work, or school?

_____

_____

_____

_____

_____

Using Your Gifts in the Celebration Service

Some will exercise their gift in the celebration service but this is not the main place to do so. Using your gift in the celebration service is the least likely place to use your gifts. I counsel churches to first test a person in the small group before allowing that person to exercise his or her gift in the worship service. The celebration gathering is mainly for those who have practiced their gifts on the smaller scale and are now ready for the larger gathering. Without being tested in a smaller gathering, the person might become nervous and stumble. If you can't give a clear teaching on a passage of scripture in the small group, for example, you most likely won't be able to teach in front of a larger gathering. It's in the cell group that we learn, have people confirm our gifts, and then are given greater responsibility before more people.

Memorize IT!
"So it is with you. Since you are eager to have spiritual gifts, try to excel in gifts that build up the church" (1 Corinthians 14:12).

Remember IT!

What principle stood out to you in this lesson?

_____

_____

_____

_____

_____

_____

Main points:

1. We should use our gifts in the presence of other people and seek their confirmation about what gifts God has given us.
2. Using a spiritual gift is always accompanied with a God-given desire to use it.
3. Spiritual gifts can be used in daily life, a small group, or a larger group gathering.

Apply IT!

1. Use your gift(s) around other people and ask them about what gift(s) they think you have.
2. Determine if you desire to exercise your spiritual gift (s).
3. Use your gifts in daily life and your small group.

How Do I Help Others Discover Their Spiritual Gifts?

Discovery can be contagious.

The discoveries of Christopher Columbus had an impact far beyond the discoveries themselves. While other discoverers had come to the new world of the Americas before Columbus, his impact and significance in history had a snowball effect. Columbus's journeys came when sailing techniques and communication made it possible to report those voyages easily throughout Western Europe. Other explorers were emboldened to set sail and to discover new land and wealth.

You don't know the impact you might have on others. When you are filled with the Holy Spirit and experience him working through you, it's inspiring. As you get excited about spiritual gifts, others will catch your excitement. As you find and discover your spiritual gifts, you'll inspire others to do the same. If you're leading a small group, you are in the perfect position to help others confirm their gifts and experiment with new ones.

Allow People to Experiment

Cell group leaders have the exceptional opportunity to inspire others in the group to step out and use their gifting. Ask Mary to bring the refreshments. See how she responds. Maybe she'll be overjoyed by the opportunity or maybe she'll bristle and make excuses. We are all called to help out, but those with the gift of helps and service will gladly offer to help.

It's a great idea to have cell members lead portions of the meeting, like welcome or worship when the cell leader is there. In this way the cell leader can give feedback to the cell member.

If during the small group meeting, you notice that Bethany, for example, worships with passion, you might want to take Bethany aside after the meeting. Ask her to pick and lead one or two songs during the next cell meeting. Discover if she's faithful in actually doing it, but then also watch how others respond to her. Be sure to compliment her, regardless of her performance. If she passes the first test, give her additional responsibility.

Try IT!

Read Matthew 14:28-29.
How do we see Peter's willingness to take risks in these verses?

_____

_____

_____

_____

_____

How can you apply these verses to help others use their gifts in the cell context?

_____

_____

_____

_____

_____

_____

Or maybe Kirk has the gift of mercy and wants to organize a social outreach to the impoverished immigrants living in the south end of town. It's okay to place the responsibility on Kirk because he initiated it. But are you willing to allow Kirk to step out and try? Kirk's attempt to use his gift of mercy will energize him and others—and will extend the kingdom of God in the process.

Granted people will make mistakes. They'll fall flat on their faces. But when they do, encourage them to get off the ground and to look up. Learning is all about making mistakes and then learning from those mistakes. Some people wait for perfection before doing anything for Jesus. With this attitude, they do very little.

Do IT!
Think about the gifting of each member in your cell. Plan to ask one or two members to exercise their gifts in or outside the cell.

Great group facilitators are open to allow people to experiment with gifts that are different from their own gifting—as long as the use of that gift edifies the rest of the group. As the leader gives members more liberty to exercise their gifts, the members will experience new freedom and commitment.

Help Others Learn About the Gift Options

I was reading one book on spiritual gifts that authoritatively affirmed that humor was a spiritual gift. Now, I love a great joke as much as anyone, and I admire those who have a brilliant sense of humor. But humor as a spiritual gift? Where in the Bible does it say that humor is a spiritual gift? I just don't see it, and I'd be very cautious to promote such a gift. Even though the Bible is the final authority on spiritual gifts, there are also some great books that I'd recommend (see appendix 2).

George Barna, a Christian researcher, took a survey in 1995 to determine how many believers knew their spiritual gifting. At that time, 4% of born again Christian believers said they did not have a spiritual gift. Yet just five years later, that percentage had shot up to 21%. And in that same survey, the way people described their spiritual gift was quite wrong (e.g., being a likeable person, patience, survival skills, etc.).[1]

This gap in knowledge will surely grow wider unless we help people to:

1. Understand what the spiritual gifts are.
2. Identify their own gifts.
3. Confirm the gifts they do have.
4. Encourage them to exercise and develop their gifts

A great idea is to prepare a cell lesson on spiritual gifts. But make sure that it's not just a Bible teaching time. Make sure that you give people an opportunity to identify their own spiritual gifts. Ask them why they believe they have such and such a gift.

As preparation for a cell lesson on the gifts of the Spirit, have the members read the passages on the gifts of the Spirit. The three main passages are Romans 12, 1 Corinthians 12, and Ephesians 4. Scripture is the first place we need to look.

Spiritual Gifts Lesson for Cell Group

1. Read Romans 12:3–8 and 1 Corinthians 12:4–11.
2. What kind of teaching have you had on spiritual gifts in the past?
3. Why does God give spiritual gifts to the church?
   (answer: for the edification of the body)
4. What gift stands out as the one(s) that you might have? Why?
5. How do you determine what spiritual gift(s) you have?
   (answer; desire, testing the gift, confirmation by others)
6. How can you use your gift in the cell context?

---

[1] Barna Research Group, "Awareness of Spiritual Gifts is Changing," news release, February 5, 2001, pp. 1-2.

Try IT!

Reread Romans 12:3-8; Ephesians 4:7-11 and 1 Corinthians 12:4-11, 27-31.
Think of each person in your cell group. Based on your observations of these cell members, make a list of the gift(s) you think each person has.

_____

_____

_____

_____

_____

_____

Personal Desire

Richard Nelson Bolles first self-published the book *What Color is Your Parachute* in 1970. The first printing sold one hundred copies. Little by little people began to recommend the book, and now, thirty-six editions later, it has sold nine million copies. It all started when Bolles, as an ordained Episcopal priest, lost his job in a budget crunch. He discovered that many of his fellow ministers shared the same predicament: their jobs were in peril, and they had no idea what to do. So Bolles did some research and wrote a 168-page guide to help ministers find jobs and change careers.

At the heart of Bolles's formula for finding the right job are two questions:

1. What do you want to do?
2. Where do you want to do it?

Notice the theme of desire. What do you want to do? This is also where the search for gifts starts. What do you really like to do? The gifting God has given a person will stir up a feeling of joy and pleasure when using that particular gift. God knows that we won't last long at something that doesn't stir our imaginations and pump us to the highest level.

Look for the seeds of desire in those you are helping in the process of discovery. Look for the light in their eyes as they serve, teach, evangelize, or pray with people for healing.

If someone continues to volunteer for the same thing, there's a good chance that God has placed the spiritual desire within. Confirm that desire and challenge the person to pursue it. If a person loves to spend time with others while offering counsel, most likely that person has the gift of counseling. Let the person know that he or she is appreciated for the counseling efforts. Your job, then, is to encourage the person within that particular gifting.

Try IT!

According to the list you made in the last exercise, ask each person in your cell if he or she desires to use the particular gift that you wrote down.

If yes, this might be the confirmation the person needs to start exercising that particular gift.

If no, most likely the person doesn't have that particular gift.

Confirm the Gift

Why don't you become the first person to try to confirm someone else's gift in the group? You've read through this book, and you've grappled with the gifts of the Spirit. Now, it's your turn to help someone else discover his or her spiritual gifts. Perhaps you could say to Jim, "I've noticed that you were great at explaining that passage of scripture. Perhaps you have the gift of teaching?" Maybe Jim has never even thought about this possibility. Or perhaps Jim doesn't even know what the spiritual gifts are. You can help encourage Jim in this way.

As you begin to see spiritual gifts in others, God will use you to encourage them. Perhaps Phyllis receives a lot of impressions from the Lord. She likes to say, "The Lord was showing me that he's going to start converting people to Jesus, so let's be ready." You sense that

Phyllis has the gift of prophesy. You could say to her, "Phyllis, has it ever occurred to you that you have the gift of prophesy? I'd just like to encourage you to step out and believe that God has given you this gift."

Memorize IT!
"For this reason I remind you to fan into flame the gift of God, which is in you through the laying on of my hands" (2 Timothy 1:6).

Remember IT!

What was the main truth you learned from this lesson?

_____

_____

_____

_____

_____

Main points:

1. We need to encourage cell members to step out and use their spiritual gifts even though they will make mistakes in the process.
2. Knowledge of the spiritual gifts, personal desire, and confirmation from others open up the doors for individuals to use their spiritual gifts.

Apply IT!

1. Encourage people in the cell group to step out and exercise their spiritual gifts.
2. Go to someone who you believe has a particular spiritual gift. Ask that person whether he or she has such and such a gift.
3. Provide resources (e.g., books, spiritual gift tests, etc. which you can find referenced in the appendix) to help people determine their spiritual giftedness.

How to Coach Someone Using this Material

Many churches will teach this material in a group setting. This is the normal way to use the material, but it's not the only way. If you choose to teach a group of people, outlines and PowerPoints are available on CD for the advanced training books, *Discover* and *Coach*, as well as all five books of the Basic equipping series. This CD can be purchased at www. joelcomiskeygroup.com or by calling 1-888-344-CELL.

Another way to train someone is to allow the person to complete each lesson individually and then ask someone of the same gender to coach him or her. The coach would hold the "trainee" responsible to complete the lesson and share what he or she is learning.

I believe in multiple methods for teaching material. The fact is that not everyone can attend group-training meetings. But the person still needs training. Coaching is a great option.

Coaching the Trainee through the Material

Ideally, the coach will meet with the trainee after each lesson. At times, however, the trainee will complete more than one lesson and the coach will combine those lessons when they meet together.

The coach is a person who has already gone through the material and is now helping someone else in the training process. Additionally a coach must have:

- a close walk with Jesus.
- a willing, helpful, and gentle spirit. The coach doesn't need to be a "teacher." The book itself is the teacher—the coach simply holds the trainee accountable with asking questions and prayerful encouragement.

I recommend my book, *How to Be a Great Cell Group Coach*, for additional understanding of the coaching process (this book can also be purchased on the JCG web site or by calling 1-888-344 CELL). The principles in *How to Be a Great Cell Group Coach* apply not only to coaching cell leaders but also to coaching a trainee. I recommend the following principles:

• Receive from God. The coach must receive illumination from Jesus through prayer so he has something of value to give to the trainee.

• Listen to the person. The coach's job is to listen to the trainee's answers. The coach should also listen to the trainee's joys, struggles, and prayer concerns.

• Encourage the trainee. Often the best thing the coach can do is point out areas of strength. I tell coaches to be a fanatic for encouragement. We all know our failures and have far too much condemnation hanging over us. Encouragement will help the trainee press on and look forward to each lesson. Try to start each lesson by pointing out something positive about the person or about what he or she is doing.

• Care for the person. The person might be struggling with something above and beyond the lesson. The material might bring out that specific problematic area. The best coaches are willing to touch those areas of deep need through prayer and counsel. And it's one hundred percent acceptable for the coach to simply say, "I don't have an answer for your dilemma right now, but I know someone who does." The coach can then go to his or her own coach to find the answer and bring it back the next week.

• Develop/train the person. Hopefully the person has already read the lesson. The goal of the coach is to facilitate the learning process by asking specific questions about the lesson.

• Strategize with the trainee. The coach's job is to hold the trainee accountable to complete the next lesson and/or finish the current one. The coach's main role is to help the trainee sustain the pace and get the most out of the material.

• Challenge the person. Some think that caring is good but confronting is wrong. The word care-fronting combines the two and is what the Bible promotes. If we truly care, we'll confront. The Spirit might show you areas in the trainee's life that need to come under the Lordship of Christ. The best approach is to ask for permission. You might say, "Tom, may I have permission to speak to you about something I'm noticing?" After the person gives you permission, you can then tell him what the Lord is laying on your heart.

First Session

When the coach meets with the trainee, the Holy Spirit will guide the session. Creativity and flexibility should reign. I do recommend, however, the following principles:

● Get to know the person. A great way to start is to use the Quaker questions. This will help you to warm up to each other. After the first week, the coach can open in prayer and simply ask about the trainee's life (e.g., family, work, studies, spiritual growth, etc.)

Quaker questions
1. Where did you live between the ages of 7-12?
2. How many brothers and sisters did you have?
3. What form of transportation did your family use?
4. Whom did you feel closest to during those years?

● Be transparent. Since you've already completed this training material, share your experiences with the trainee. Transparency goes a long way. Great coaches share both victories and struggles.

"Coaching Questions" to Use Each Week

A great coach asks lots of questions and listens intently. The goal is to draw the answers from the trainee so that he or she applies the material to daily living. Key questions to ask each time are:
1. What did you like best about the lesson(s)?
2. What did you like least about the lesson(s)?
3. What did you not understand?
4. What did you learn about God that you didn't know previously?
5. What do you personally need to do about it?

The coach doesn't have to ask each of the above questions, but it is good to get into a pattern, so the trainee knows what to expect each week.

Pattern to Follow Each Week:
1. Prepare yourself spiritually before the session begins.
2. Read the lesson in advance, remembering the thoughts and questions you had when you went through the material.
3. Start the session in prayer.
4. Ask the coaching questions.
5. Trust the Holy Spirit to mold and shape the trainee.
6. Close in prayer.

Are There Additional Spiritual Gifts?

How many gifts are there? The Bible lists at least twenty gifts in the New Testament, but some people include Old Testament gifts, such as craftsmanship. The twenty gifts of the New Testament are listed in three major biblical passages: Ephesians 4, Romans 12 and 1 Corinthians 12–14. Because Paul was the author of all three passages, he repeated the similar gifts in all three passages, but he also introduced new ones in distinct passages.

The fact that Paul introduced new gifts to distinct churches during a particular time period has caused many—like myself— to conclude that Paul was simply identifying particular gifts, not declaring that only certain gifts existed.

In this book, I've decided to take the safe route and only cover those twenty gifts that are specifically mentioned in the New Testament. Yet I believe in the very real possibility that there are additional gifts, either not mentioned specifically in these gift passages or not mentioned in the Bible.

Writers on the gifts of the Spirit have differing opinions on the number of these additional spiritual gifts. My two favorite authors on spiritual gifts--Peter Wagner and Christian Schwarz--both take the liberty to add additional gifts such as celibacy, hospitality, missionary, prayer, exorcism, voluntary poverty, martyrdom, craftsmanship, artistic creativity, and music.

The number of gifts a person comes up with really depends on how that person defines charismata, and the breadth of their interpretation. My point is that we should allow for flexibility when defining the spiritual gifts and remain open for the Holy Spirit to reveal additional gifts.

OTHER POSSIBLE GIFTS	KEY WORDS	DESIRES	SERVES BY
Celibacy (1 Cor. 7:32–35)	Content being single	To freely serve	Remaining single
Hospitality (1 Peter 4:9)	Hosting for God	To open home	Openness
Missionary (1 Cor. 9: 19–23)	Cross-cultural	Serve ethnic groups	Leaving own culture
Intercessory prayer (Luke 11:1–13)	Prayer warrior	Intercede	Praying
Exorcism (Luke 10:17–20)	Deliverance from evil	Cast out demons	Exorcising
Voluntary poverty (Acts 4:32–37)	Give away all	Identify with the poor	Simple lifestyle
Martyrdom (Acts 7:54–60)	Martyr	Die for Christ	Death
Craftsmanship (Ex. 30:22–31)	Building	Constructing things for God	Building projects
Artistic creativity (Ex. 31:1–11)	Creativity	Create art for God	Creative art
Music (1 Sam.16:14–23)	Music	Worship God	Worshipping

Books

There are many excellent books on the spiritual gifts. I recommend:

- Peter Wagner's book *Discover Your Spiritual Gifts* (Ventura, CA: Regal, 2005). Wagner's book has been updated many, many times and is still a classic.
- Christian Shwarz, *Three Colors of Ministry* (St. Charles, IL: ChurchSmart Resources, 2001). Shwarz's books are practical and thorough.
- Bryan Carraway, *Spiritual Gifts* (Enumclaw, WA: Pleasant Word, 2005). This book is both enlightening and comprehensive.

- Joel Comiskey, *The Spirit-filled Small Group* (Grand Rapids, MI: Chosen Books, 2005). This book is specifically directed to the operation of the gifts in the context of the small group.
- Craig S. Keener, *Gift and Giver: The Holy Spirit for Today* (Grand Rapids, MI: Baker Books, 2001). This book explores the biblical background of the spiritual gifts.

Spiritual gift discovery is such an important aspect of ministry that I strongly recommend all the reading possible. Since each part of the body of Christ is formed by individual gifts, we need to give careful attention to what each gift is.

Gift Tests

Gift tests can help confirm your spiritual gift. Some of the gift tests, however, also assume that the participant has substantial experience in ministry and can answer questions that involve ministry assessment. Those who are new in the faith often don't have that background.

Perhaps the two most popular gift surveys are Peter Wagner's gift survey and Dr. Carbonell's survey and DISC analysis. Some others are listed below:

- C. Peter Wagner's gift survey called *Finding Your Spiritual Gifts* (Ventura, CA: Regal, 2005). Web site: www.regalbooks.com
- Dr. Mel Carbonell's gift survey that features a gift inventory and the DISC personality evaluation. Contact: 1-800-501-0490 or www.uniquelyyou.com (published by Uniquely You, Inc.).
- Alvin J. Vander Griend's gift survey (developed and published by the Christian Reformed Church, CRC Publications). Contact: 1-800-4-JUDSON.
- Paul Ford's gift survey (published by ChurchSmart Resources). Contact: 1-800-253-4276.
- Christian Schwarz's gift survey (published by ChurchSmart Resources). Contact: 1-800-253-4276.

Just remember that more important than spiritual gift tests is practicing your gifts and receiving confirmation from others in your small group or the church at large.

Just remember that more important than spiritual gift tests is practicing your gifts and receiving confirmation from others in your small group or the church at large.

Does God Give the Gifts Permanently?

Much debate about spiritual gifts revolves around whether God gives believers more or less "permanent" gifts or whether God gives "temporary" gifts as the need arises. The view that God gives permanent gifts is called the constitutional view. The situational view, on the other hand, teaches that spiritual gifting is given spontaneously to meet a particular need.

Constitutional View of the Gifts

The constitutional view of the gifts is the "traditional" view that teaches that all have a particular gift or gifts, and that we need to discover that gifting. Since the gifts of God remain permanently in the believer, the job of each Christian is to discover and utilize each God-given gifting.

Various authors and researchers have dedicated their lives to help believers discover what particular gifts they already possess. Through spiritual gift surveys, believers are encouraged to discover the exact gifts they have been given, according to the constitutional gift of the Spirit survey.

I agree to a large extent with this view. It does seem as if God has given us at least one grace gift (1 Peter 4:10) and believers are exhorted to use their particular grace gift (Romans 12:4). The human body analogy with its different parts is often used in scripture to highlight the diversity of gifts. Since body parts are permanent, it would seem that gifts have a similar characteristic. God has given us particular gifts of the Spirit and then calls us to use those gifts.

Situational View of the Gifts

According to the situational view of the gifts of the Spirit, God doesn't give any one particular gift to anyone. Rather, God simply distributes the gifts of the Spirit according to the needs that exist. For example, if someone needs healing, God might decide at that moment to distribute the gift of healing to someone in order to pray for healing. According to this view, all gifts reside with the Creator, and he decides when a particular gift should be given for the good of his church. 1 Corinthians 14:1 says, "Follow the way of love and eagerly desire spiritual gifts …" This verse seems to indicate that God wants us to desire spiritual gifts, even above and beyond the ones that we possess at the new birth.

I also like this view because there is a tendency to think, "this is my gift" rather than this is the Spirit's gift that he has given me to bless the body of Christ.

The tendency for those living in individualistic, western societies is to interpret the gift passages as related to individuals. Yet, the Spirit is primarily concerned about the group—in contrast to the individual—and he endows the charismata on the Church. The reason that individuals are given free grace in the form of gifts is to bless and edify Christ's church.

The situational view of the gifts creates a greater expectation for the Holy Spirit to work in new, exciting ways—rather than, for instance, to wait for Harry who has the gift of tongues and always delivers his gift at 10:15 A.M. on Sunday morning. The situational view also frees believers from operating only in one or two gifts and not expecting to be used in any other.

Combination View

The combination view says that God has given each born-again believer at least one or more gift. And in this sense we need to discover what he has placed in us. Yet, the combination view also realizes that God is the gift giver, and that he reserves the right to drop any gift into our lives at anytime. We need to expect God to work in our lives at all times.

I personally believe that each believe has one or more permanent gifts. Yet, I also think that God wants us to be open to receive new gifts at any time, as the situation calls for it. God loves to do new, amazing things in us.

Expect God to Move

The Scriptures exhort the believer to desire spiritual gifts (1 Corinthians 14:1). Paul even implied that it was acceptable to desire certain gifts above others (such as, prophecy over tongues). The issue of desire flows into the idea of expectancy. Not only should the believer desire spiritual gifts, but he should also expect God to manifest those gifts. Because it's clear from scripture that the Holy Spirit wants this to take place in his Church, the next step is to expect him to do so.

I once talked to a group of pastors about spiritual gifts. Some were actively practicing all the spiritual gifts, while others were very cautious due to past experiences. Despite their differences, however, the one thing everyone agreed upon was the need to expect God to work. Active participation in the spiritual gifts creates an expectancy that God is working. Unfortunately, expectancy is a missing piece in many small groups and churches. Long ago weary leaders gave up on expecting God to work.

In *The Message*, Eugene Peterson interprets Ephesians 3:20–21 like this, "God can do anything, you know—far more than you could ever imagine or guess or request in your wildest dreams! He does it not by pushing us around but by working within us, his Spirit deeply and gently within us."

Today we need God's divine guidance more than ever. Now is the moment we need the gifts of the Spirit to flow through us in a mighty way. Expect great things from God and then attempt great things for God. As you step out in the things that God has shown, he'll show you even greater works than you can ever imagine.

Index

CPSIA information can be obtained at www.ICGtesting.com
Printed in the USA
BVOW082231130912

300233BV00007B/13/P